JUMBO

Vocal Selections

ISBN 0-7935-9070-1

WILLIAMSON MUSIC®

A RODGERS AND HAMMERSTEIN COMPANY

www.williamsonmusic.com

EXCLUSIVELY DISTRIBUTED BY

HAL•LEONARD®
CORPORATION

7777 W. BLUEMOUND RD. P.O. BOX 13819 MILWAUKEE, WI 53213

T0050917

JUMBO

Vocal Selections

The Circus on Parade

Words by LORENZ HART
Music by RICHARD RODGERS

REFRAIN

Hold your hoss, here they come, Rat - tat - tat goes the drum. The

cir - cus is on pa - rade._____ See the clown fall - ing

down, It's the best show in town. The cir - cus is on pa -

rade,_____ See the monk climb the rope, Hear the steam cal - li-

Diavolo

Words by LORENZ HART
Music by RICHARD RODGERS

REFRAIN

Diavolo: Di - a - vo-lo, the thrill king, Di -

a - vo-lo is still king, With no

fear of death he keeps clear of death Zoom - ing thru the

air. Di - a - vo-lo, the fear -

bove, Nerves tense ____ and mus-cles tight a - bove.

Perched on ____ his diz - zy height a - bove *Men: Stead - y!*

Stead - y! *Are you read - y?* *Diavolo:* Di - a - vo - lo, they're

breath - less; Di - a - vo - lo, you're death -

less; Spot- lights catch you up like a stat- ue up there.

Men: Who re - mem - bers Dan Cos - tel - lo great - est of them all, poor fel - low.

Diavolo: Laugh at death

Di - a-vo-lo! _____ Di- _____

Little Girl Blue

Words by LORENZ HART
Music by RICHARD RODGERS

Sit there and count your fin-gers, what can you do? Old girl, you're

through. Sit there and count your lit-tle fin-gers, Un-

The cir-cus tent was strung with ev-'ry star in the sky A-bove the ring I loved so well;

Now the young world has grown old,

Gone are the tin-sel and gold.

D.S. al Fine

The Most Beautiful Girl in the World

Words by LORENZ HART
Music by RICHARD RODGERS

REFRAIN

The most beau - ti - ful girl in the world _____ Picks my ties out,

eats my can - dy, Drinks my bran - dy, _____ The most beau - ti - ful

girl in the world. _____ The most beau - ti - ful

star in the world _____ is - n't Gar - bo, Is - n't Diet - rich

My Romance

Words by LORENZ HART
Music by RICHARD RODGERS

REFRAIN

My ro - mance does-n't have to have a moon in the sky, My ro-

mance does-n't need a blue la-goon stand-ing by; No month of

May, no twin - kling stars, no hide a - way, no

soft gui - tars. My ro - mance does-n't need a cas-tle

Over and Over Again

Words by LORENZ HART
Music by RICHARD RODGERS

gain. A star does not come out of the sky, He starts to

work at ten._____ To reach the top you've got to keep

try - ing o - ver and o - ver a - gain._____

TRIO

Up in the morn-ing and down in the ring a - cro-bat, rid - er and